Hickory Station

Hickory Station

Poems

Adrian Rice

Press 53
Winston-Salem

Press 53, LLC
PO Box 30314
Winston-Salem, NC 27130

First Edition

Cover design by Kevin Morgan Watson

Cover photograph and back cover photograph,
Copyright © 2015 by Alan Mearns,
used by permission of the artist.

Author photo by Jon Eckard, Eckard Photographic.
www.eckardphotographic.com

Printed on acid-free paper
ISBN 978-1-941209-32-5

For

Ross Wilson & Alan Mearns

Brothers-in-Art

and

In memory of my dad

Kenneth Robert Rice
(1938-2014)

A Note from the Publisher

Since the author of this book hails from Northern Ireland, and this book will be distributed worldwide, the editor has chosen to honor the rules of United Kingdom grammar and punctuation to preserve the voice and spirit of the author and his work. No words have been Americanized by removing a "u" or changing an "s" to a "z"; likewise, commas and periods have been left outside the quotation marks, in spite of it irritating the editor when U.S. authors do this.

Acknowledgements

The author and the publisher gratefully acknowledge the following for previous hospitality to some of these poems:

"Breath" was published in *The Asheville Poetry Review*

"Song" was selected for Winston-Salem Writers' 'Poetry in Plain Sight' poster project

"Back In" first appeared in *Iodine Poetry Journal*

"The Apologist" was published in *Poetry Ireland Review*

"Sometimes I Think", "Little Things", "Recognition", and "Roman" first appeared in *FourXFour Poetry Journal*

"Hobo", "Nature", and "The Electric Life" were published in *A Poetry Congeries with John Hoppenthaler: July 2015* (Connotation Press.com)

"So Lovely to Hear the Rain" appeared in the Rain Issue of *Bloodshot Journal of Contemporary Culture*, Spring 2015 (Amaranth Press, NC)

"Hickory Haiku" was first published in 2010 as a chapbook by Finishing Line Press

A small selection from "Texts" appeared in *The Clock Flower* (Press 53, 2013)

"The Right Word" was published in *Voices: 25 Years of The Pushkin Trust* (Pushkin Trust, 2013)

Some of the poems were broadcast on *Wordplay* with Jeff Davis (Asheville FM)

A Note from the Author

The author would like to thank some significant encouragers: Sacha Abercorn (The Duchess of Abercorn), Ian Adamson, Joseph Bathanti, Martin Beattie, Gerard Beirne, Charlie Bishoff, Patrick Bizarro, Jackie Braun, George Bryan, The Captain's Bookshelf (Asheville), Bud Caywood, Marion Clarke, Patricia Craig, Harriet Custer, Paul Custer, Gene & Kelly DeMaegd, Colin Dardis, Jeff Davis, Patrick Joseph Dorrian, Mike Dowdy, Ian Duhig, Ramona Fletcher, Keith Flynn, Omair Rabbini & Caitlin Guinn, Eric Hart, Rebecca Hart, Brian Houston, Margaret Gregor, Brenda J. Graham, Bob Hinkle, Ryan Johnston, Mel McMahon, Virginia McKinley (and staff of Malaprops Bookstore, Asheville), Alan Mearns, Vachel Miller, Elliott Millinor, Chrisanne & Lamar Mitchell, L Nelson Moretz, Kathleen Murphy, Arlene Neal, Betty O'Hearn, John & Betty Orr, Micki Paul, Rebecca Pierre, Martin Quinn, Anne Rawson, Matthew Rice (my poet-son), Marylou Roddy, Richard Rankin Russell, Davóg Rynne, Ari Sigal, Angela Beaver Simmons, Brenda Culp Smith, Sandy & Mike Stevenson, Don Talley, Woodrow Trathen & Dorothy Maguire, Ross Wilson, John Womack, Craig R. Wyant, and especially Kevin Morgan Watson ('The Boss') at the peerless Press 53.

Love, as always, to Molly & Micah, and to my beloved family back home in Northern Ireland.

Contents

II. Hickory Haiku

III. The Kingdom of Porch

IV. Texts

V. From Abroad

The Poetry Porch

for Molly & Micah

My driver's window is open to the world
As I sit at the fumy crossroads waiting
For the lights to shift from red to green.
A loud crack sets off a car alarm behind
Me in the car park of Lowes. The thunder
Thief is back. Sky shoulders boast black cloud

Epaulettes. Weather wars are about to blow.
It seems like the lights are stuck on red,
In league with the angry god above.
I'm sinking in the humid heat, when my eye's
Taken by a white cherry blossom by
The roadside, celebrating in the frisky wind,

Shedding party petals like there's no tomorrow.
The Japanese know them as flowers of death,
Living and dying in a blinding show.
I am grateful for the persistence of
Whiteness in the sunless dark, as they pepper
The Blazer with their papery buckshot.

Just as I'm about to put up the window,
Just as things are about to change from stop to go,
A single blossom comes straight for me and
Lands a soft, pure touch on my Irish nose.
So, I carry its white kiss home and pass it on,
To you, through this page from the poetry porch.

I ran out in a summer dawn into the voices of birds, and I
returned, but between the two moments I created my work.

from 'In Szetejnie' by Czeslaw Milosz

For here, as nowhere else on earth,
Men were brought together for a moment
At the beginning or end
Of their innumerable journeys,
Here one saw their greetings and farewells,
Here, in a single instant,
One got the entire picture of the human destiny.
Men came and went, they passed and vanished,
And all were moving through the moments of their
lives
To death,
All made small tickings in the sound of time –

from 'The Railroad Station' by Thomas Wolfe

I.

Hereabouts

Snowman

for Mike and Sandy Stevenson

We went to sleep in the Appalachian cold
and woke up to an almighty downfall,
snow falling fast like so many hyphens
and dashes shook from sky's packed page.
Cabin-bound, missing our mountain-town
book launch, we happed and Wellied-up

to fashion our first family snowman.
With a pipe made from frozen snow-snot –
boasting a perfectly shaped icicle cone –
and head-helmeted with a white baking bowl,
he was the cut of a weird winter Nazi,
a comically redeemable version

of something the opposite of comedy …
I wondered what the universal Lord felt,
looking down on our glove-handed efforts.
That maybe we were a chip off the old block,
making a figure of snow in our own image?
When the sun rose rampant the next morning,

it didn't take too long for our snowman to melt.

Breath

What is death,
but a letting go
of breath?

One of the last
things he did
was to blow up

the children's balloons
for the birthday party,
joking and mock-cursing

as he struggled
to tie all
those futtery teats.

Then he flicked them
into the air
for the children

to fight over.
Some of them
survived the party,

and were still there
after the funeral,
in every room of the house,

bobbing around
mockingly
in the least draft.

She thought about
murdering them
with her sharpest knife,

each loud pop
an angry bullet
from her heart.

Instead, in the quietness
that followed her
children's sleep,

she patiently gathered
them all up,
slowly undoing

each raggedy nipple,
and, one by one, she took his
last breaths into her mouth.

What is life,
but a drawing in
of breath?

Without Warning

Comes on without warning, the ache of Eden,
That soul-longing for the wholeness we all lack.

It may be no more than a learned delusion,
Or evidence of something we will win back.

Psalm

A robin lights on the tree stump
Sloped like a lectern,
And sings his morning psalm
To the sun after rain.

Already at their early chores,
Busy comrades flit back
And forth on the soil shore,
Surfing the corrugated

Waves of the vegetable patch.
The old couple who still sow so,
Sit silent, content to be scarecrows
Who scare nobody off.

Mid-Air

With other porch-roof
trophies hung,
the praying mantis doesn't
have a prayer,

wrapped up
in an invisible cocoon
by a little spider,
in mid-air.

Trick

Books are piling
up around him,

each a paper brick.
Someday, soon, they'll

finally wall him in.
He's been building

these paper walls since
early adolescence.

He's still convinced
that, one fine day, they'll

do the trick.

Mercy

Back from the community
college and haunted
by the face of the young
boy with siblings in tow,

walking the roadside dirt
in the sulphurous heat,
manfully struggling
to shepherd them home,

worry filling his face
looking towards the adults
haunting the rundown
porch he's headed for.

O Lord, Most High,
have mercy on our souls,
for the Kingdom of Heaven
is surely his!

The Hanging Heart Chart

of evening's anatomy

is not as black
as the truest Blues

but washed with Burton's
white melancholy

being somewhere between
those pillared extremes

of sure-I-never-knew-ya
and deep topophilia

while the disembodied
voice announcing

the football fortunes
of the Red Tornadoes

comes and goes like bad
reception on mountain radios

and the dogs are crowing
and the birds are clicking

their fingers and thumbs
and cicadas are background

radiation from some big bang
and rose bulbs need changing

and house lights are too bright
and cars fly by too loud and too fast

and there's Einstein riding
bitch, smiling, like

he knows what IT means
and I gotta get outta my house

pants and into my jeans
and someone has touched down

'cause I can hear the screams

Bookmark

You left us first, and then those books, behind.
    – Seamus Heaney, 'An Afterwards'

Sitting alone in the Crescent Moon Café,
blowing the last keg of Harpoon IPA,
I was thinking that even though I think

it matters, I don't just judge a book
by its cover, but by how many slivers
I have to tear – like some reverse origami

or litmus test (I swear, if they could,
they'd change colour inside there) –
from the solitary bookmark that I've slipped

inside the newfound book to keep my place,
to mark the pages that I want to re-read
and share with my wife, my oldest son, my friend,

and with everyone. But sometimes, sometimes,
one stingily shredded bookmark isn't quite
enough to keep score of a great book's gems –

like now, which provides a bookmarked space,
and somehow leads to these captured lines
that strangely leave even that good book behind.

Simplify, Simplify

From the hearth to the field is a great distance.
    – Henry David Thoreau, *Walden*

The Indian life is surely best.

It shouldn't be so surprising
that Thoreau had no need
to wander the whole globe
to sense what is wrong with us.

He only had to go not much
more than the length of himself –
but three or four miles from his
birthplace – to build his cabin by

the pond, and get what he wanted
to fill his famous Journal. Now it's
much more difficult to even try to
simplify. So many die soulless in a

blaze of activity. But still – and it is
a true American thing – I only have to
go three or four paces from the hearth
to the porch to fetch my poems.

The Indian life is surely best.

Nailed

My boy won't let me
cut his nails anymore.
Although he says he wants
to be like our good friend –
his right hand religiously

ravened for the classical guitar –
I think he's maybe lying.
I think he's really afraid
that I will hurt him, nip him,
as I fear I may have done,

peering through poor reading
glasses from the Dollar Store
or wielding blunt clipper blades
like a lazy butcher.
So, I've been trying

to reassure him, every day,
that he will be OK,
that I'll be extra gentle,
but he backs away in fear,
both hands hid behind his back,

saying, *I have no hands*.
Last night, I managed to cut
one full hand while he slept
on the sofa, but hadn't the heart
to cut the other, seeing him

suddenly surface from deep sleep
into wide awake, speechless horror.
Then, today, we came to an agreement,

to cut just one nail, daily.
I cut today's, but now he wants

his mummy to cut tomorrow's.
Did I hurt him, again? I thought
I'd nailed it. O the joys of parental
paranoia … Sometimes it's hard
to accept even nail-clipping failure,

and hard to share the familial load,
even with your beloved wife, his mother.

For Us to Share

I get to walk my son to school and back
each weekday, weather permitting, and each

day, on our way home, he stops to select
a leaf and a tree nut, the fallen kind

that drop on sidewalks and parked cars this time
of year, and I urge him to go gentle

with the leaf, and he always asks me, *Why?*
I say, it's beautiful, but it's brittle,

and easily destroyed. So he carries
it home each day like it is the last leaf

left for us to share in the whole wide world.

When No One

The long habit of living indisposeth us for dying.
– Thomas Browne, 1643

On the night when no one can work,
it must be how we feel when we
have put off doing our work

until the very last minute, and are
suddenly full of that night before,
last minute panic to get something

done, something we've had days
or weeks or months or even years
to finish, to successfully complete,

but now the dreaded deadline
has finally, really – really – arrived,
and we are found willing, but wanting,

on the night when no one can work.

Song

I was close to sawing
some leafless limbs

from the dogwood tree
when, right on cue,

a robust robin
appeared on one

and sent its soul out
across the lawn.

So, I let them be,
since even a barren

bough can hold a song.

The Lab

It is good to sit in and look out on Lexington Ave.
In experimental Asheville, the foothills of the sky,
Where locals and visitors march to an alternative

Beat. But today, in The Lab, smoke-free diners discover
That there's an interesting game of inches underway
Involving a couple of young Ashevillian lovers

Who have sneakily slung the leggy ladders of themselves,
Armed with American Spirit, over the street-side lip
Of the summer patio to roll-up and sit some spells.

And, while dangling their rogue cigarettes out over the wall
Of the bar, they're sailing big colonial smoke-clouds back
Towards fellow diners, who – once nothing more than virtual

Strangers – are now happy to be finding themselves binding
Together like a libertarian citizenry,
Brow-cocked, bulls-eye hot, firing looks and purse-lipped *pfff* warning

Shots across the sociable sea to defiantly say –
In experimental Asheville, the foothills of the sky,
Such monkey business is an unacceptable cliché.

Lovers

Lovers, or so they seemed to be,
strolled out of Malaprop's Bookstore
and around the corner,

descending one of the many hills
of the artistic city,
holding hands as they went

on their downward way,
swinging their hands, as lovers do,
clasped hands locked into

a human swing-seat
fit for one or two invisible
children that might grow

from their romantic sway.
Just another momentary image
from another Ashevillian day.

Wordless

for Molly

I know we were
on a great day out,
and only parting
for an agreed
hour or two,
but I would rather,
really, have stayed
with you and him,
to watch you
shoot pinball together

in the Asheville Arcade,
than to be rolling down
Walnut Street, fancy-free,
on my way to graze
in Downtown Books,
and onwards to curry
our carryout from
marvellous Mela ...
for I didn't like
the sudden feeling

that I was already gone,
and that you two,
so much younger,
were the only family left ...
it's true, that even
for the likes of me,
a relentless word-hoarder,
that sometimes books
don't matter a damn.
So, love, I want

you to know,
that when it comes
to you and him –
like when you first
slid your hand
inside my jacket
and laid it on
my racing heart –
that wordless is still
the favoured flame.

Roost

In-between the showers,
our second-string balcony
gives a decent view-gap
to the breaking waves
where younglings are

trying to stand on water,
hoping to run under the furls
of those momentary boughs.
I settle in with a gentle glass
to watch the pelicans,

in liquid formation,
hurdling the front-row houses.
Ancient champions
of an airy Olympiad –
pre-Christian saviours

who, when called upon,
would tear their own
breast to save their young
with precious blood –
they're all beak and wings,

coffin-mouthed, relative
ugliness made elegant
by their gorgeous glide
and arrowed dives.
Lesser birds, pigeons huddle

on nearby roofs, some napping,
some bathing in rainy gutters,
others just landing,
each final wing-flurry
a heraldic moment,

a classic coat-of-arms.
And there's the gutsy gull,
and talented tern, even starling,
too, hustler coming from
nowhere, and taking ten

times longer to get anywhere.
And so we are back at the beach,
their kingdom, although it's us,
strung out along the strand,
who seem to think we rule the roost.

The Servant's Song

for Katie Willhelm

Setting her southern feet
on a southern strand
for the first time ever,

the simple servant girl
memorialised the ocean
in one simple line –

It just keeps flushin' all the time!

Wrapped

Perched, pelican high,
watching a pristine
Stars & Stripes
flapping wildly
in the impending

thunderstorm breeze
from off the Atlantic,
furling and unfurling
like unpredictable
waves, I realise

afresh how flags, not
unlike their various
owners, will often get
too wrapped up in
their precious selves.

Worthy

Caught without proper paper,
I'm writing this on the back
of my son's Air Blasters gun
cardboard packaging won from
the Carolina Beach Arcade,

while sitting on the Hurricane
Bar rooftop, with a view
of the amusements on one side,
the Atlantic on the other,
and a supermoon in the sky

being snapped by the many
with their adult pacifiers.
Writing about looking down
on the boardwalk Putt-Putt course
at two males proudly adorned

with matching tacky Stetsons,
and sporting, even more proudly,
matching rebel flag T-Shirts,
their kids noticeably punching
the air with their fists as they

celebrate each ugly bogey.
Writing about my eye then catching
sight of a wonderfully built
black man walking past Putt-Putt
with a serene smile on his face,

and wearing a T-shirt with
the one word slogan – 'WORTHY'.
Overhead, as I pay my tab,
pelicans patrol the promenade with
something still approaching innocence.

Back In

While seabirds soar and collapse their wings,
Raining like folded umbrellas into the foam,

We rush-bag the customary beach stuff
And skedaddle from the threatening rain.

Someone has surely laid hands on the earth-globe.
Soundside trees shiver and rear like frightened foals

As another storm wipes the sky board clean,
Leaving it a watery wash, streaky with lightning.

Time to shower and sup and top-deck long enough
For the clouds and moon and stars to be worked back in.

Current

Our current century's connectedness-cum-disconnectedness
Via the cell phone was no more apparent than at Carolina Beach

When, instead of bikini-clad goddesses emerging from the sea
With slick knives tucked inside their skin-tight bikini bottoms, we

Were presented with preoccupied women who were afraid to flirt at
All with the tide, for fear they'd get their delicately tucked cellulars wet ...

While, on the one hundred degree holiday strand, the molten metal
Mobiles were never too hot for any sun-screening humans to handle ...

Still, I must stop whingeing on and on and on like it's some big deal,
Since, as my young friend believes, I might as well boycott the wheel.

The Signing

Setting was tasteful,
flame-dark,
almost theatrical.

He read his little heart out.

Afterwards,
they handed him
some books to sign,

destined for the shelf,
each one courteously spread
for his fountain pen.

He sat there, smiling,
at the candlelit table;
each and every signature

a kind condolence to himself.

So Lovely To Hear the Rain

So lovely
to hear the rain
against the house

in the booky silence
gentling those
watery pebbles

romantically
at the window
to remind me

of how lucky
it is to be
on the inside

and not out
to be in the here
and the now

So lovely
to hear the rain
against the house

Bare Necessities

It's a perfect photograph, my screen
saver, taken, as always, by his doting
mother: my little boy, elfing his way
across the seven-one-seven lawn

with nothing but Diego underpants
on his Irish-white frame, both arms
outspread, legs scissoring, lead toe
pointing skyward in summer flight.

His face is a commercial for smiling.
He reminds me of Kipling's Mowgli,
mimicking the elephants marching.
So I guess that makes me big Baloo,

the brassy bear. Look, there I am,
lying on my back, using the river
as a drifting waterbed; and there
he is, straddling my hairy belly,

tickling me and laughing his heart out.
(Shere Khan is nowhere to be seen.)
In a wasteful world, built on greed,
simple bare necessities are all we need.

A Little Lower

I've missed you, solitary angle-poise,
Lamp that bends to my silent, littered noise,
Stooping low in inanimate prayer,
Shedding light on optimistic paper.

That bigger star has been gladly shut down,
The Betelgeuse of this late night work room.
So, take the throne of your desk-given place,
A little lower than my half-lit face.

Knowledge

Sometimes we can lose
those closest to us
not to death
but to life
to a project that
doesn't include us in it
(well, maybe, not enough)

to a room inside the other
that only they can enter
to a life that has
ten thousand things
with them only at its centre
to a country that simply
is too far for us

to ever visit ever
to another person
another love
that deserves
all their attention
Sometimes it's simply
like that

though it's seldom
ever simple
but for our own
heart's sake
let us determine
that such knowledge
is somehow ample

Grief

Calling repeatedly
for an absent mate,

a single red bird will
be autumn's last leaf.

Gone

Though their lights
still reach us,
leading us on,

our memories

are like stars
that have long
since gone.

Sometimes I Think

Sometimes I think that my happiest days
Have been spent in bookshops;
Especially when everything's in bloom,

When the trees have hung out
Their flags on every street,
And the clouds have gone AWOL

Or been safely penned
By that orange collie of the skies:
It's then that I'm in my element

Because, because there's magic in the book.
Even Hewitt, custodian of reason,
Was moved to heresy as he took me

By the elbow in his house
To tour his library, his working collection,
And pointed to a buckramed book

On the jam-packed shelves. *See this one?*
Believe it or not, and I sense you will,
Roberta and I were in Edinburgh,

And as we hurried past a second-hand
Bookshop, I suddenly stopped and said
That I needed, quickly, to go in.

I knew, somehow I just knew,
That there was a book on the shelf
That was somehow meant for me.

So we entered, and I went straight
To it, reached for it, and took it.
Now, that's all that I can tell you.

It was there. And it was for me.
My friend always says that we should
Choose our addictions well.

I think I have. Only time will tell.

Amen

for Leonard Cohen

The humble master,
Crooked as a question mark,
Crooning the answer.

Otherwise

It took until my fiftieth year
To fully realise
How quietly heroic
Old people often are –
How hard it is for them
To still press on
With hope, without despair.

And then to further realise
Just how mock-heroic
Young people often are
For much of their loud lives –
Although, the truth to tell,
As the old know full well,
The young know otherwise.

Heavy

sunset
diluting
orange

moonrise
cuff-linked
chaperone

sibling
of our seething star
crooning

O
heavy
is
the
world
for
those
who
bear
its
weight

Image

In the darkened room
He lies underwater –

An image negative
Dipped by unseen hands –

And holds his breath.
He emerges, steps out,

And dries himself off,
A fully developed man.

Advice to a Young Poet

If you've any
ambition,
lose it early.

For what's
ambition worth,
if you're here

to tell the truth?

To Memorise

after MR

Before heading to bed,
Before cancelling
The back room light,

Too tired to play pick up,
I take a long look at the path
I must take across the floor

Through my son's toy debris
And into the hallway
(Adorned, would you believe,

With the same floral wallpaper
Of my grandparent's hallway
In the home where I started).

I close my eyes to memorise
My whereabouts in the certain
Dark. Then set out.

Little Things

Sometimes things seem a little less lonely,
Turning my eyes to the starry prairie,

Seeing the old familiar Plough still there,
Part of my America. Only here,

Folk have always known it as the Big Dipper,
And that makes things even lonelier.

Sleep

I felt I had to tear myself away
from the midnight screen page
and go downstairs to see my boy,
but when I got there
he had fallen asleep
on the sofa, freshly fetal,
while watching *Alice in
Wonderland* on his own.
It nearly broke my heart.
But I hoped he had slipped

into his own wonderland.
And I hoped his mummy
had done the same in her slumber
in the bedroom, back upstairs.
For sleep is inherently holy,
at least for those who are lucky,
for those without much care.
And how much more for those who
crave a moment, a measure, of peace?
For women who somehow suffer

their so-called husbands
for every dangerous second
of every inherently unholy day.
For children who suffer their warring
parents for every second of every
tension-filled night at the family home;
who fear their fathers coming
home from a late night out,
reeking of old smoke, stale beer.
Sleep's a suspension of belief,

and disbelief, a blessed holiday
from the everyday ... or, I know,
a dream reel of everything unholy
that happens to an innocent person,
or may never happen, but happens
to them in sleepy time, anyway:
packed with phantasmagoria,
with every computation of human
horror imaginable to us ...
Still, the pluses outweigh,

bringing some soothing even
to the insomniac, that bastard child
of night (of day?), that brother/
sister of the unsociable hours ...
Either way, I wish my son had been awake,
been wide-eyed, and full of talk. But then
I wouldn't have sat down to write.
Wouldn't have followed that big
white rabbit down the rabbit hole.
I wouldn't have fallen into this poem.

Reflection

Slow-driving down 127 on the routine road to Food Lion
(Though I'm never sure whether that should be down or up),
Vacantly lost in the travelling, enjoying a break from thought,
I window re-see what used to be one of our popular bars:
A pool-playing, dartists' paradise, the venerable Sgt Peppers.

It's now a Goth-fonted church building named Reflection –
An unforeseeable change of hands in such irreligious times
(Though I shouldn't be surprised by the buckle of the Belt).
I've been dwelling in Eliade's *The Sacred and the Profane*,
Pondering his talk about the nature of human relationships

To space   and time   and nature   and the cosmos,
And I now find myself totally thinking – are the spaces
That once housed churches much happier to be bars?
Or are spaces that once held bars happier to host churches?
Suspicion being, the 'mysterium fascinans' is: spatially, same.

Harold

in memory of H.T. Roddy (1924-2013)

It's Gastonia, and it's Sunday.
Raindrops crater the windscreen.
Sirens moan like mating cats.
Things are rundown and rained on.
Like parts of Belfast, but with heat.

We squeak into the car park
Of the Brian Center for Care
To take our chances with Granddaddy.
Conifers umbrella the car,
Saving us from a downpour.

We get out and go in. It's like
Casting a full-blown scene from
'The Regions of Sin':
Immobiles like blanched whales;
People with barely enough skin

To cover the bone; long-life lifers,
Diabetes-deformed; lung-challenged
Old folk, still cancer-sticked,
Chair-free at the Care Center door.
We know the room we are looking for.

We hold our breath, smile the corridor,
Almost hold our noses, too.
We reach his room, double-check,
Then dander in all bonhomie,
Hoping Harold knows it's we.

Husband, truck driver, card-shark, Granddaddy!
Sit up in bed and tell us the score!
Sometimes it's surprisingly good, like normal:
Others, it's playing tigtag with the past,
Unsure how long each memory will last.

50

But Molly loves to go with him,
Milk every word for all it is worth;
Even when something sounds hurtful,
Every exchange is ladled with love.
Memory at all is song of the dove.

Harold, I cherish the days I sat on the sofa
Across from your big chair in the trailer
And chewed the fat over Tiger and Phil
Or Junior and Tony and The Intimidator –
My American 'Billy' and me in front of TV.

Now you seem to remember very little.
Or is it everything? Sundowners
Dawns on you every time the disc drops.
Dementia's the word on no one's lips.
Our loving family trinity,

Marylou and Molly and Michelle,
Will see you through until the end,
Then carry your ashes to the wished-for sea:
The sea I'm glad that I crossed over to find
Your granddaughter, and to be your friend.

Rocked

Looking out through glass
crosses the brightest streetlight
between my neighbours' houses
which lights the bare old trees

that I can see right
through to the late night
half-moon lying on its back
like the wheel-less body

of a pearly pram – a silver stroller –
a Christmas crib – a coracle docked –
cradling the dark half of itself,
an unseen something,

waiting to be rocked.

Rise and Fall

Rainstick rise
And fall of cicada chorus

Southern storm is
Coming for us

Will turn our trees
To rainstick forest

Turning Away

turning away from
the snapping turtle
of the screen
he scans blue noodles
under his skin
thinking – and when
can the fumble
be blamed on the rain?

he remembers the strand
a furrowed brow
wet with the tears
of an absent sea
and the golden sun
set like the creamy yolk
of a Cadbury's egg

and those carpeted stairs
fanned like the pages
of a beige book
screaming
the worm is round
and closer to the ground

he closes his eyes
goes into what isn't him
but is where
he comes from
and still does

descending the marble
keyboard of the stairs
he sends wet lightning
into the shivering pale

toilet paper
hanging in the bowl
like a jellyfish

he sees the trees,
Earth's eyelashes

fluttering, fluttering, flootering on

Testing

Drumming my collarbone,
lying down to relax,

like the doctor had drummed
on my chest and my back;

knocking on the lintel,
sounding the bone,

testing the scaffold
of my mortal home.

Designer

for John Orr

When sunlight dawns
Shadow turns on
An anchor for them
To nowhere firm

Fact from fiction
Is hard to learn

Faced with the Earth
(Its roundy shelf)
They square the circle
And build their house

Designer sits
Quiet as a mouse

Stable

Time to stabilise
His world;

Let go of him,
Release the hold.

And there he goes!

Pedalling for all
He's worth.

The bicycle tilted
On its axis

Like the Earth.

On

in memory of Neil Armstrong (1930-2012)

Armstrong, Armstrong, Armstrong, even Armstrong's gone!
And we, who have never been much farther than

Our own front door, are suddenly the poorer
For losing the man who first tippy-toed on

Our dusty old moon in graceful gravity,
And then kept himself to himself forever

After. Hard to fathom his humility.
If it had have been us, we'd have gone on, and on,

And on, and on, and on, and on, and on, and
On

Somehow

I

was walking, one way,
against what seemed
like the stream of humanity

flooding the Underground,
when it suddenly dawned
on me that I had, somehow, found

you

Soundside

for Mary Rowe

Suitably emerald wetlands;
Young crows in the crow's nests
Of earthed aerials strung

Like some old ship's rigging;
High-flown jets and speedboats
Zooming their frothy contrails;

Cloud choirs congregating
To lead the evening worship
Of water, the primal parent.

Top-decked, up with the tree-sway,
Bird-eyed, dove-call comforted,
My chosen tablets are *Self-Reliance*,

High Lonesome and *Parnassus* from
The bookshelf lucky bags of home.
This is the spot where the sun sets,

The soundside, paradoxically silent,
Holding its lake-like own against
The seaside's surfable commotion;

So quiet I can almost hear the well-wish
The sun makes as it drops into the beyond.
Now to sit, caberneted, to watch supermoon

Build a Stonehenge of shadow until dawn.

Peace

for Richard Rankin Russell

The delicate child
who enters the room,
almost innocently,

at that very moment
when the elders
are at each other's

emotional throats;
who draws them
from off of themselves

and onto each other
just as every little thing's
enough to make them

finally break and put on
their care less coats,
is called Poetry.

Death of the Book

Night-time reading
is like eating
late-night cheese –

it gives you dreams.
After reading
about the death

of the book,
I dreamed
I pitched a tent

on my own
in the mountains
back home –

a giant book
angled above me,
the floor a

bed of pulp.
I lay there,
nose-hairs strummed

by book-smell,
looking up
at the page walls,

at words made
visible by
the moon bulb.

When I woke,
in the dream,
the sun was out,

and the words
were nowhere
to be seen.

The page walls
were as blank
as vacant screens.

Games

Letting go.
Last looks.
Last things.

Like the last time
we lay our heads down
in the same house

as the same family.
All that epic stuff.
But what about when

we turn our back
on the chemistry set
and the magic set?

Or on the swivel
of Subbeto players
and their emerald pitch?

Or on the plastic
skate-board-based GIs
and Cowboys and Indians

and the bugled Cavalry?
Or on parental Monopoly,
Cluedo, Battleships?

Or on the Snakes and Ladders,
futtery Tiddlywinks,
those dog-eared playing cards,

proud Chess and granda Draughts –
on all that compendium of games!
But, most of all,

what about the last time
we lift the football
from the evening pitch

trapping, toeing, flipping
it up into our hands
and bringing it back

into the lit up house,
lobbing it to the box-room corner,
rolling it to the foot of the bed,

smell of the grass still on it,
smell of the summer air
still fresh on us,

and then unthinkingly
heading back down
the stairs to woof

some tea and toast
not knowing that
the end of an era

has come, the end
of our glorious childhood
career of sports,

that no amount
of adult footy
or parkland jinx

or playing Daddy
with our kids
can ever fix?

Informed Worship

for CS

Say it all began with a hot big bang.
Imagine that.

The helter-skelter of cosmic rush
Relaxes into a palm's push

For our wet and wonderful world,
Which rest-rolls,

Like a sacred blue lottery ball,
Across the cold, occult black.

Say it all began with a hot big bang.
Say it with a universal amen.

In the End

for Padraig McGuinness

In the end, it all comes
Down to something like this:

Water beads on a thirsty branch,
The giddy glide of birds,

The greenness of grass,
The elderly neighbours drifting smilingly past.

The Great Table

In the silent semi-dark,
while working at the words,
I reached to backhand-brush

what I thought were cookie
crumbs from the cover of
Faithful and Virtuous Night

by the poet Louise Glück,
and was startled to realise
that I was trying to erase

the stars of The Milky Way
from the cover photograph.
One day, perhaps, that's how

the Maker will clean off
those cosmic crumbs from
the great table of the Universe.

Recognition

The buds are beginning to open,
the young leaves are on their way.
Soon they'll be giving me
their green full-handed waves.
I would love to just stand here
at this upstairs window

and watch them as they grow.
But I know, even if I stood here
for a full day, without blinking,
I would still miss everything,
I would still not be a party
to their supernatural way.

Which makes me remember
that's how life always is.
We don't notice people growing
when we're travelling with them.
It's only separation which lends
recognition, the shock of decay.

The deal-with-the-devil of the émigré.

II.

Hickory Haiku

Hickory Haiku

for Chrisanne and Lamar
& Georgia and Stewart

Providing a home
from home – our necessary,
neighbourly angels.

I

Fiftieth birthday:
musings between here and there,
there and back again.

II

We Irish aren't wooed
by weather: but, for folk here,
it's a love affair.

III

Carolina clouds ...
icebergs of air ... solar suds ...
pageant procession.

IV

Like poets, they've no
collective noun ... let's say, a
flurry of squirrels.

V

Sam's Club girl shakes my
hand, says: *You're the first Ireland*
that I've ever met!

VI

Valley Hills shopping
mall: women wear their new-found
breasts like 1st rosettes.

VII

Our budding dogwood
whispers: *Wait till you see me
in pink blossomhood ...*

VIII

Night-winds lay the corn
rows low. Morning, they rise –
foals finding their feet.

IX

Olde Hickory Tap
Room: draught handles are beer-bows
which target the Thirst.

X

Shadows from the tree
limbs burgle our neighbour's car –
ringwraith moonlight mime.

XI

Full-faced moon-gazing ...
I love how s/he dwells in
approachable light.

XII

Carolina Beach:
moonlit beer-caps on midnight
sand – redneck sea-shells!

XIII

Rollicked in wee waves –
Step right up, see the wonder!
The Human Flounder!

XIV

Beach-bum day well spent.
We wish the sun's bronze coin in-
to the Atlantic.

XV

Famous, world-wide, for
Welcome! Southern & Irish
hospitalities.

XVI

Like, so unlikely –
'The Unlikely Poet' gets
Key to the City!

XVII

Our mountain wedding –
the wind rose, filling the sails
of our holy vows.

XVIII

Moll's curves meander
like a sleepy river on
a hot summer's eve ...

XIX

The sun's done gone. Dark
ink surges through sky water –
a storm's a-comin'!

XX

Merciless, moaning
winds do shake the daylight leaves
off of autumn trees.

XXI

Tombstones in front yards:
bodies hung from trees – Hallo'
ween in Hickory!

XXII

O elderly moon,
a lidless eye blurred by a
cloudy cataract.

XXIII

Camel crickets rest
on the dusty, starlit floor
like lunar modules.

XXIV

Invading our space,
carpenter bees hover – come
and go. UFOs!

XXV

You've written yourself
out. Now, write yourself back in
again, Adrian.

XXVI

Two contrails cross in
the royal sky – the airy,
brave flag of Scotland.

XXVII

Like found poems, the bare
necessities of home – Heinz
beans & Weetabix!

XXVIII

Snoopy sees egrets
blossom on golf courses like
white water lilies.

XXIX

A 'Flying Tiger',
Moll's great-uncle Fred's love of
golf is love of flight.

XXX

'No Alcoholic
Damage' – puke prohibition
in Memphis taxis.

XXXI

I feel good, I knew
that I would, now to have a
first dream in colour.

XXXII

Belfast storage has
arrived! I swerve and swoop, book-
to-book, swallow-eyed.

XXXIII

Last bookcases up –
solar ray panels giving
more mental science.

XXXIV

There is always one
dog that barks a background to
the birdsong of thought.

XXXV

I'd die a little
nightly from sleep apnea –
CPAP breathed new life.

XXXVI

Bittersweet pillars
of melancholy: holy
opportunities.

XXXVII

Cell phones are legion –
techno mobiles hung over
our modern mangers.

XXXVIII

Compared to that for
the mocha, the wait for the
book is much shorter.

XXXIX

Harleys sputter past
me – shades of biker brothers,
Arran and Annesley.

XL

Same the world over –
the smug freemasonry of
the mediocre.

XLI

Out of work ...... means play ...
means thoughts ... means words ... means play with
words ... means poems ...... means work!

XLII

We whinny and neigh,
two rocking horses grazing
the pasture of porch.

XLIII

Ungentle redbreasts,
these regimental robins
sure boss the bird-ground.

XLIV

Night trains clippety-
clop through downtown Hickory –
The Tornado Trot.

XLV

Nature's risky here.
Nothing's poisonous back home …
except some people.

XLVI

The ISS rocks!
From 'out there', we've already
disappeared from 'here'.

XLVII

Hubble rendezvous –
Canadarm reaches up and
grabs the Stanley Cup.

XLVIII

Atlantis holding
the Hubble high: the Hubble-
huggers' last goodbye.

XLIX

Cemetery short-
cut ... the otherworldly weight
of that strange estate.

L

Seven-One-Seven,
on Fourth Avenue North West –
Hickory heaven.

III.

The Kingdom of Porch

Dominion

Just as easily, I could
have elected to sit
in the half-lit
downtown tavern,
or lounge in the soft sofa
wine shop on the square,
conscience polar clear,
being blessed by
my working wife,
busy putting her players
*through their pre-*Antigone
agonies at the Tractor Shed Theatre;
but I chose, instead, to perch,
once again, on the porch,
among the happy families
of robins and blue jays,
cardinals and doves,
listening to their necessary
chitterings; soaking in
the stoic wisdom
of trees and shrubs.
And then I realised,
like for the first real time,
that they are all in our care –
all in our care –
and that dark word
came back to rock
me in my chair.

I. The Silent Page

The late afternoon cheap cabernet has surprising legs.
Porch railings are horizontal white ladders.
Maddened wasps climb in and out of the airy slats.
Birds are clapping to a close on the neighbour's lawn.

Cumulous crown the blue. Everything's in early bloom.
Leaves and petals announce themselves colourfully again.
Difficult not to see humans as being the least beautiful
Things on the avenue today, with our cares and greeds,

Our feints and foibles. As soft evening arrives,
For the very first time someone is practicing
Scales in my porched earshot, on, of all unearthly
Earth-based things, a blooming tuba.

(A 'chuba', as we'd say back home,
Returning the 'tu' to 'chu', as we tend to do.)
Soon the scales change to 'Frère Jacque', and it's
Hard not to feel that someone has it in for my monkish self.

Especially when they lose interest in their own sounds.
But then it stops, and I turn the yellow porch light on.
My hand and its shadow-puppet, with the nib as nose,
Skiffs slowly, once more, across the silent page.

II. Hidden

I have always had one foot
in the field, the other on the street,
so the front door balcony's

a happy halfway house for me,
a redeemable version
of being hidden in plain sight.

Tonight, I have wallowed
in the aerial acrobats,
those silent crisscrossers,

crazy loop-lappers, gobs full of bugs.
And now I'm noticing how
the bright roses are suddenly

turned off at sundown,
even before the soft light
is up, leaving everything green

to be more than seen, to be felt.
I know that we need sunlight
to prosper, but we dare not

neglect the benefits of dusk,
when the moon lies its lovely, tilted
head down on the night's blue bed.

III. Open Space

Unusually, the avenue's full of children,
Racing here and there with happy screams.
I'll just sit tight. Soon they'll be drawn
Inside to supper in front of screens.

And when they are, the avenue's fuller
Now that it's almost empty, now that there's
Only the inplaceness of curtained houses
And the silent patience of planted things.

I love this porch, this open space, this
Rented window on the world. Candle flames
Flicker in the faintest wind, side-stepping
Their reflections in their pools of wax.

'Meet me at the corner where two trees meet'
Is the given line that's keeping me taxed.
As darkness rises, I suddenly imagine
Myself gluing fireflies to my fingers for light.

IV. Hobo

for Kevin Todd

So buried in a book
I almost missed them

But I looked up
Just in time to see

Two classic lines of sunlight
Tracking our neighbour's yard

And how the hobo in me
Ran to jump the train

That rode such rails
Just as they disappeared

V. Heresiarch

Endeavouring to settle down to read the freshly amazoned *Irresolute Heresiarch*, a lit-religious take on my beloved Milosz, trying to get the pronunciation right in my head, and on my tongue, of a book with a subtitle for the critical ages – *Catholicism, Gnosticism and Paganism in the poetry of Czeslaw Milosz* – I leave my porch station for just a second to go fetch some evening wine, when the doorbell rings behind me (doorbells don't ring on 4th Ave NW – this isn't old Ireland), and I reopen the door to a lanky youth, picture-tagged, back-satcheled, foldered, who says, *You must be the father of the house. I am that, I guess*, I reply. He continues talking, but I don't comprehend a single word that follows, and embarrassedly summon my (American) wife to come take over.

Evidently, he wants to sit down with us to discuss something vague about how we might help the local community. My wife, a passionate, peerless, beleaguered educator, up to her ears in toddler, and her eyes in cooking late evening chops, uncharacteristically, but politely, says that we're both teachers, and therefore do more than enough for our community. So the young man leaves.

As we cross paths on my way back outside, my wife asks if I know the boy. *I wouldn't know him from Adam.* She about chokes. *That was Adam!* She says. *What?* I reply. *His name was Adam!*

Later, as darkness drops, I see him slope off along the far side of the road, hugging his folder, waving weakly, wandering out of sight beyond the neighbour's rose garden.

VI. Shadow

Likely it will happen but once,
so nothing like looking
up from the teatime porch
to see with shock and awe
a huge hawk cruising
the neighbour's lawn,

window-high, a low-flying
jumbo jetliner gone
strangely astray along
suburban streets (though one
should know that
it's forever more at

home among the foliaged
streets than us) then turning
right to glide straight up the
middle of the road – a runway it
did not need to land on –
to the T-Junction, then lifting

itself effortlessly, silently,
smokelessly above the houses
and their proud trees, and away.
The entire blooded garden
life I saw from then to dark
had the shadow of survivor.

VII. Like Someone

Looking out
across the avenue
to the neighbour's
banked-up leaf-curb,
I see a path-gap

has appeared
in the middle
of the perfect pile,
and there stands
two big robins –

I mean, King Robins
like someone
has just parted
for them
a reddish sea.

VIII. There Is a Line

for SF

There is a line that I can't get out of my head,
Since it showed up several nights ago.

On a balmy evening, in-between rain,
I wish to rest my eyes on the darkening trees,

Their heavy-laden leaves still turned in.
I want to sit and take it dropping slow.

Repose on the porch and read, not scrawl.
But the line in question won't let me go:

'The comedian has said in his heart
That there is no God.'

IX. The Way Home

for ASM

I chose to walk rather than hitch a ride,
and no sooner had we parted on the street outside
the Moon, not more than a minute from your

gentle parting jibe – *ack sure,*
you'll probably find a wee poem
on your dander home –

I strode into a firefly guard of honour.
Those matchless passers of the flame
lit my Oakwood stroll with their

royal relay the whole way back,
and stayed outside the door
until I got myself slippered-up

and seated on the dusky porch.
Then, one by one, as if on cue,
they each turned off their golden torch.

X. Nature

Nature never wears a mean appearance.
    – Ralph Waldo Emerson ('On Nature')

Just when you think
you have clinched the deal
on that certain equilibrium
which some of us mere mortals
seem doomed to seek –
sitting in the porch-shade
on a steamy afternoon,
with the wee man sat happily
in his garden sandbox –
a big bumblebee steers
straight for you at an unnatural
speed, and then won't go away.
So, you find yourself belting
it irritably out of your porch-space
with the full-handed back
of a Bill Stafford poetry book –
an exemplary pacifist –
to the old Belfast tune of
Get the hell out of here!
Blushing, flustered, you then
return to the book,
feeling silly, a little guilty,
certainly less than mature,
back to that elusive goal
of being fully one with other
humans, and with nature.

XI. Promised

for Karen and Bruce Anderson

Lovely how the rose holds the light,
especially those magnificent magenta ones
in full-bunch-bloom behind the old Marine's
white picket fence, a fence that looks more

like the foot of a giant's four-poster
than like anything else: so the roses
are quite literally in a flower bed,
each a voluptuous still life,

their velvety cups brimming over,
filling every available inch of air.
Folksy-perfect, the patriarchal slogan –
I PROMISED HER A ROSE GARDEN

XII. This Far

The evening avenue is psalmist-still.
There's not one single breath of breeze
To trouble the tall sails of the trees.

The main road is now the main deck,
And the porch is a hung-up lifeboat
For the mind, and the body, and soul.

Everything else rooted is peculiarly calm:
Each blade of grass, each honeysuckle,
Each molten-marvelous garden rose.

The only things which are still moving
Are the bugs and birds, and all those
Rolling by in the huff and puff

Of passing cars. With my welcome wife,
And my youngest son, I am content to be,
So to speak, so completely lost at sea

On yet another liquid lap around our
Mid-life star. And I am constantly
Grateful to have ever come this far.

XIII. Another

Another hot evening on the poem porch,
The verse veranda, and as much as I love
The Devil's Ivy that was draping its

Leafy locks from the banister, it's been taken
Back indoors to unclutter the view,
Because I don't want to miss seeing anything ...

Like that robin who's wiping his beak
On the red brick arcing the flower bed,
The way my granda sharpened knife blades

On sandstone like he was spreading butter back
And forth across a batch of supper toast ...
Another memory found that once was lost.

XIV. Last Light

Last light. Luminous avenue.
Trees radiating their deepest greens.
Leafy sky-divers, ripened branches

Breast the lifting winds.
Surely spring is the best.
Coming on against all the odds.

The timely, temporal return.
Indisputable rebirth.
(Though it's hard not to notice,

Again, that very little
Ever grows straight.)
The electric suns turn on.

Human star factory.
Our Oakwood nebula.
Downtown trains sound

Their nightly yawps.
Birds babble before bed.
Only time they get

To unwind before
Their sleep of the just.
I'll join them, not too long

Before they get back up.
Storm's been rumoured.
There's the lightning.

The thunder's on trust.

XV. The Electric Life

Night after night,
I feared they'd left me,
decided to drop me
like an old flame.
Each evening, near dusk,
their courting time,
I studied the tall trees
outlined like coastlines
against the blue,
their blue gaps
like lakes or loughs,
and waited. But nothing.

Then, the other evening,
I saw something
in the treetops,
not golden-green
but white light,
blinking on and off,
that I mistook for planes,
but which was them.
Were they starting
in the heavens,
where they normally finish,
and working down?
Or were they simply
being newborn?
They were still
so much better
than the predicted
meteor shower,
being living light,
not inanimate matter
borrowing fire from
our atmosphere.

And then, tonight,
while I'm glowing
with Birkert's book,
they've returned,
in all their glory, playing
peek-a-boo with my eyes,
so many of them sailing
slowly around the porch
like gentle Zeppelins,
close enough to touch.
This is the life.
The real electric life.

XVI. Timely

Timely rain this evening
has driven mowing neighbours
from the springtime avenue,

falling down just hard enough
to soften leaf-light cymbals
in the orchestra of trees,

and dapple the dry surface
of the old sun-blistered road,
each sizzling raindrop playing

out a game of touch and go.
Falling down with ample weight
to help the hungry robins

tempt some hidden worms onto
their top tables made of lawn;
to tease parched red roses with

gentle moist-lipped promises
of overflowing cupfuls,
and pearl the blooming saplings

that glisten in leaving light,
just like young women posing
on their Graduation night.

XVII. Fireworks

First time I've seen it happen,
right below the porch parapet,

a robin sailing in to take
a firefly, just as it flamed,

the bird's mouth suddenly
starlit in the growing gloom.

Though one light has undoubtedly
gone out, they won't despair,

for there's plenty more of nature's
fireworks ready for their display.

XVIII. For Mearnsy, Who Said He'd Scream
If I Mentioned Clover or Fireflies Again

Always a shock to go from the conditioned-cool
To the oven-blast, when you're going from inside
To out; not an experience native to home.

When I park myself on the porch in my chair that
Feels under-heated hot, as in your swanky car,
It's like all the other chairs, the adopted cat,

The grill, the trees, telephone poles, drivewayed cars,
All we are members of a buddy-boy sauna.
Looking out, Alan, I almost expect to see

Clovers towelling themselves off. The tarmac must be
Blistering. The birds are strangely quiet. This climate,
Only the cicada is king. And yes, you've guessed,

On evenings like this, I can't help but notice
Those fireflies are decidedly energetic ...
I sip warm wine and await your panegyric.

XIX. Just

Just rained for all
of fifteen seconds,

something sudden
arriving from

somewhere else,
bringing sound

with its wetness.
Never known it

to rain so little,
so drop and go:

like dribbles from
incontinent clouds,

or lippy overflows
from brimming

sky-baths whose taps
have been turned off,

just in time.

XX. The Old Trees

Like dolmens round my childhood, the old people.
– John Montague

Like dolmens round our houses, the old trees,
Each rooted to a designated spot;
None of them holding any real aces,
With birthplace, and graveyard, dealt out by rote.
Yes, it's here that they'll have to live, and die,
And nowhere else. Yet they own the 'profound' –
That being silently satisfied with one's life.
Fully clothed, or naked, they stand their ground.
Patient circle of leaf leviathans –
Who only wave their skyward tails in storms
When the clouds burst, and the winds have risen,
And the air is thick with floodable rain –
They stay strong through moving generations,
And none of them ever seem to complain.

XXI. Away In the Head

The doves have shown up.
They sit in fours on the high wires,
And coo at these lines.
I'm thinking about The Poet

Being 'away in the head',
About just how true that is,
And not as a put-down, but praise.
Better to be away in the head

Than one of the hollow men.
And then I reach for my porch pen
To write a cheque out to *Poetry*.
But how does one – me – pay Poetry?

O let me count the ways!
O let me count the days!
Hey, should Poetry not pay me?
I know, I know, now I'm just being silly.

The doves rise up like a round
Of applause and reel off.
I really must get the head down
To all of that other stuff.

XXII. Volley

for Joshua Presnell

A volley of automatic
gunfire going off –
a first for the porch –
then the wind-scythe

of a helicopter overhead.
Then the automatic
reminder to myself –
that as long as I can

hear it, I am still safe.
Sure, it's as natural
as slipping on a pair
of worn Irish brogues.

For it matters not
how the years add up –
old nerves still ripple
the back of the other net.

XXIII. Loss

It isn't the same
without the fireflies.
It just plain ain't.

Like Nature's power
bill has not been paid,
or her miniature bulbs

have all blown at once.
It might be how the world
will feel – if it can last

that long, which it can't –
when all the sky stars
have disappeared,

because everything,
as we know, is hurtling
away from everything else,

and the end of all things
material is loneliness.
Even Christ's sky was

brighter than ours,
and ours won't last forever.
Still, though nothing earthly

lasts, the fireflies will
return next summer to briefly
ease my sense of loss.

XXIV. Wasps

On an unseasonably
warm afternoon
I am back on the porch,
and the little wasps
are trying to build
in the hollow arms and legs
of my aluminum chair.

They're determined,
as they are every spring,
to inhabit my chosen seat,
but I have soaked
their sought for portals
with gasoline, being equally
determined to stay put.

But on they come,
at regular intervals,
in ones and twos only,
as if one sometimes needs
the second as witness to carry
the story of occupation back
to the others, to be believed.

I wonder what they think of me,
and feel sorry for them,
almost guilty, even imagining
the dark openings they seek
as being cave mouths
in which they wish to store
some valuable scrolls.

So I am kind to myself,
reminding myself
that it's my chair, my porch,

though I can hear them protesting
But we were here first!
Fair enough. But no matter.
For I have a porch thirst.

Gasoline will win the day,
for another year, anyway,
and I will sit safely and securely
behind my slatted battlements,
scratching the pale page
hoping, as always, to be
stung by poetry.

XXV. Word, Word

I'm sure that some of them
think to themselves, as they
pass by his porch of an evening

on their ritual doggy travels –
as they peek up at the man sat
with his face in a book or gazing

into the dropping darkness –
that little amuses the innocent.
And little do they know how

much he'd hope that that was true.
And I'm sure that they often wonder
why he stays put there, even after

the fireflies have virtually disappeared.
But it's then, it's then, that words
will flare-flame within his waking head –

here a word, there a word,
everywhere
a word, word –

showing themselves to one another,
and lightning the hidden lines that
somehow, strangely, needs be said.

XXVI. Zapper

for Paul Durcan

Almost couchant on the porch,
goggling the eye-candy
of our freshly mown yard,
fighting the thought
that so many of my favourite
things are no more than
professional killing machines,
when a gentle garden redcoat
does some floppy mid-air karate
to take down an ambling bug.

As I instinctively avert my gaze,
swivelling the periscope of my showered
head, a ginger tabby pads its way
onto the road and hunkers down,
tail slowly sweeping the sun-warmed tarmac,
eyes lasering in on another robin
plying its own murderous trade
on the cleanly shaven lawn.
And so I rise up to scupper
the tabby's deadly intent.

But then comes the first ever
avenue sound of a bug zapper!
Least that's what I'm calling it,
for now; a phosphorescent slab of light,
luminating near the garage doors
of the old Marine's house opposite:
a sinister contraption, a perilous attraction,
reminiscent of Kubrick's obelisk
that so enchanted chimps. This one
fries every bug that gravitates too close.
A white hole, if I've ever seen one.
It's a killing ground over there.
A perpetual evening electric chair.

Sometimes, Paul, it's all too hard to thole –
almost enough to drive one to thon crystal meth –
that in the midst of this silver sliver of life,
we are always so much in league with death.

XXVII. Everything Is Going to Be All Right

for Derek Mahon

The Mountains are wearing grey wigs.
Rain clouds are hanging their drapes.
Down here, it's hot and dry.
Cicadas are back.
Night-waves for the land-locked.

I'm Piedmont-porched.
I've been away for a few days,
Head-down in the books,
Wrestling with Morgan's
'Interests, Conflict, and Power'.

(An American comma
After 'Conflict' – not ours.)
But now I'm back on the street.
Back at the real work. The poesy.
A couple of nights ago,

A bubble-blow of fireflies
Meterored my study window,
As if they were signalling me
To come out to play – like we
Did with wee torches in our day –

As if they had missed me as much
As I had missed them.
And now, tonight, they're putting on
A display. Some of them even
Rounding the porch like they're

Anointing it with light ....
Everything is going to be all right.

IV.

Texts

Texts

for Alan Mearns

Just sieving the daily dust, panning for poems ...
Sent

Last night, the whole forest
moved and shook itself
like a huge drenched dog.
Sent

The leaves are looking so leafy today.
Soon, they'll change their colours, and go away.
Sent

... all night, skin-tight, hold-warm,
sheet-surf rippling and rolling
towards the coasts of love ...
Sent

It doesn't matter
how vast it is 'out there'.
We all know the 'in here'
is vaster.
Sent

With all this galactic free-for-all going on,
it's nice to live in the habitable zone.
Sent

Friendly fireflies in the garden gloom
... what dangers are they warning me of?
Sent

Rising and falling
on the chest-swells,
our wee one sleeps on
love-liners, human oceans.
Sent

Tornadoes: wind-ropes,
shower-room towels,
for real.
Sent

Night sheets
are dune-ribbed sands,
high Himalayan ranges.
Sent

There's no place left for me at the Mall
since Walden Books just up and left.
Sent

I love those late night
living room light bulbs,
those insomnia suns.
Sent

Creation critics constantly take
the proverbial piss. Apt that the echo
of our original big bang
should sound so much like a hiss.
Sent

O comforting book tent bivouac on the bedside table!
Sent

Don't beat yourself up,
relax, stay cool.
Keep your back
to stuff
that makes
the mediocracy drool.
Sent

The difference between *spending* time
and *using* time ...
Sent

The music, the wine, the glass,
the table, the flat floor,
are all mysterious
no matter how much
they explain them to us.
Sent

Bookmark-bereft, I use my watch
to keep my place for when the time is right.
Sent

It's dark, but what's
'missing' in the Universe
truly matters ...
works just as well
for what's left out
of one good verse.
Sent

The lonely eye roams the open sky-prairies ...
Sent

The apple fell on Newton's head,
the plucking of which had opened
the door of knowledge.
What a drop of cosmic luck!
Sent

Strange things happen when you're tired.
Today, for instance, I shouted out,
Who's using the hot water?
in a house that I knew was empty.
Sent

Maybe dying lets you inhabit
memory in a full way ...
Sent

Ah, astronomers and the night sky!
Those visual athletes!
Intelligent adults get to play
a big game of 'join the dots'.
Sent

Orion's not a belt, it's a butterfly.
Sent

No matter what the poets say,
leaves can't speak.
But if they could,
what would they say?
They'd tell us not to look
beyond today.
Sent

Does everything earthly also yearn to go off with a bang?
Sent

Wind died down, cloud-curtains parted,
the sun broke through and lit the house up like a set.
Sent

Hard to swallow the gun-lover's dictum –
'The gun is always an innocent victim'.
Sent

Saturdays and Sundays we often lie in,
listening to the raindrops pitter on the pane.
Sent

What we see
with the naked eye
is sadly dead
light in the sky.
Sent

Three pubic hairs in the beastly bathtub 666
Sent

From the darkling porch on rainy nights,
I watch cars photocopying the glassy streets.
Sent

Skyscraper windows ... the half-lit city's DNA.
Sent

Somewhere between Pound and Williams,
nearly every thing is 'like a',
... things are seldom what they are.
Sent

Tough times. I paddle about the house
in slippers barely fit for feet.
Sent

Humility? Are we
not those who comb
around in our own
backsides cleaning up
the flotsam and jetsam
of essential fuels?
Sent

Yawn-mouths at the foot of the bed,
my very shoes are dog-tired.
Sent

When the heating sighed into life
I thought it was her,
padding across the late night landing,
as she sometimes does,
to comfort me with kindness
and with love.
Sent

If we stoop to judge a peer,
there's always a whiff
of tampering left
hanging in the air.
Sent

When calm came,
the rain rose from the roof
like nose haar from horses
still thundering at dawn.
Sent

Long live our solar orange, vitamin juiced!
Sent

On the polished graipe handle, the Irish robin sat –
a Butlin's redcoat minding kids at a summer camp.
Sent

I said, *Poetry? Poetry?*
Poetry is verbal mathematics,
the algebra of the soul! Then fled.
Sent

Crow commands the fallen sea-forts,
dark lord of crumbling castles…
Sent

Pull your eye-catching banner
across the sky, seaplane –
you're still a poor
imitation of the pelican.
Sent

What we deeply believe is right today
is often deeply wrong tomorrow –
the shifting sands of scientific inquiry ...
Sent

Too tired to deal with the fuss,
we've let the bairn bed down
in the valley of himself
between the two mountains of us.
Sent

An instant after they strike ground,
each raindrop wears a rainy crown.
Sent

Good poets are ventriloquists
And ev'ry dummy fits their fists.
Sent

Gulls dipping and diving,
feeding from friendly fingers –
Carolina kites.
Sent

I wish we could sit for a little while more,
watching the waves frill their frenzy at the shore ...
Sent

Fidelity to poetry
is such a healthy
madness.

V.

From Abroad

Hoover

A late night car zooms
in with blaring lights,
like the old Hoover
my granny pushed

across the carpeted floors
of her timber home,
driving me into corners
where I didn't want to go,

but which I knew were
safe, because I knew
that she was always
on my side despite how

it might seem otherwise.
In fond memory of her,
I still feel safe in those scary
places where I like to hide.

A Dream of Home

A white shirt pegged
to the old clothesline
out the back of our house
on Derrycoole Way

was flip-flopping
in the summer wind
when it changed into
a perfect white swan

which I somehow
captured and ferried
back into the living room
of our house

where it perched upon
the low lake of the window-
ledge and sat there staring
at the passing people

Saved

for Patrick Kavanagh

The night before, sleeping in St Jude's Guesthouse, I dreamed I was standing by the fabled Grand Canal, watching a group of French tourists laughing and taking pictures by the water's edge. As I drifted closer, a big dog swam towards the bank where I stood, looked straight at me, and said: *She's in trouble! She's in trouble! Save her! Save her!* When I woke, it was time to leave the Dub, and beat it back up to Béal Feirste on the afternoon train.

En route to Connolly Station, I bought a cheese sandwich and a can of orange Fanta from the 24-hr. Spar shop, and parked myself on the canal bench beside Paddy's commemorative poem-stone. Things soon clouded over. And it started to spit. So I parcelled up my sandwich and headed towards the little planked bridge that spans the greeny Grand Canal.

As I approached the lock – its two wooden arms painted black, and white-tipped, like magician's wands – I heard French tourists talking, and saw them taking snaps, and automatically looked down as I crossed the slippery, rain-wet wooden walkway to find a fully submerged woman, drowning, doggy-paddling under the water, in vain. I knelt, reached in to take her highest hand, and pulled her, like a rabbit from a hat, straight up and out and upright onto the walkway beside me. Shiver-shaking, holding a soggy purse in her hand, she stood in speechless shock, canal water running out of her niagarously. Then, still wordless, she squelched off across the street and forever out of sight.

Strangers rushed to pat me on my blue-denimed back. Some even took my picture. I gathered myself, unfurled a black umbrella, and made my way homeward through the teeming city centre.

Teach

for Marty Quinn

I thought of you today,
Paddy Kavanagh,

When the schoolkids
Took time away

From their outdoor recess
To rush the railings to greet me.

I tell them stories, you see,
Teach them poems.

All that crucial mythology.

Debt

Like when the wind and rain come
for you, slapping you about the bake,
and your tired-out mother,
in her heavy collared coat,
loaded down with shopping bags,
white-knuckled hands near numb,
steps in front to take the brunt,

then stops as the gale gets worse,
turning her back to the lashing
romper-rooming your skinny bones,
and opens her sodden coat to spread
round you and your younger brother
sitting chap-cheeked in the toy-like tansad
you're struggling to wheel him in.

The Milky Way Café

In Belfast, back in the day,
My mother carried a bomb

Out of The Milky Way Café,
And calmly set it down

In the middle of the path
Opposite The Belfast Telegraph.

It was destroyed by the army.
When the media asked

Just what had possessed
Her, she quickly replied:

Possessed whom?

The Apologist

Fine words from a man
From whom words come easily –
Drawn from his midnight mouth
Like a chain of silken scarves.

Sigh

I sigh a lot now.
I never used to,
But I do.

I sigh for myself,
I know,
But I also sigh

For you.

Keepsake

I.
The only thing his family left in place
Was unfashionably yellow and green,
A castle of condiments and cutlery,
With a big buttering board
That opened and closed like a drawbridge.

Or, when the cabinet doors were shut
And the buttering board was up –
An advent calendar selection box.
Or a bulky ship-in-a-bottle maybe,
Miraculous in its scullery space.

Whether or which, it was identical
To one treasured by my maternal
Grandmother, who stood unbowed
While her home was allowed
To slowly crumble about her stubborn head.

II.
Having secured his old kitchen cabinet,
Sad but glad no-one else desired it,
I'd nowhere decent to keep it stored
But in an outhouse we used as a coal-shed.
It would've been better to set it on fire,

Being left to rot, as we could never hire
Enough room to safely house a wooden memory.
Poverty robs the poor of even inanimate succour.
Only the rich have rooms for precious heirlooms.
Keepsakes kept more for money's sake

Than any kind of help for heartache.

The After Image

for Billy

I have recorded the last time I saw
Him through the pane. But that's not how I saw
Him for the very last time in the flesh,
Though what form of flesh is anyone's guess.
I saw him passing by as clear as day,
Walking from his front door to the coal-shed,
Holding his fireside shovel out ahead
Of him, as if it were another day,
An ordinary Sunday afternoon,
Out fetching coal to heat his living room.
Normally, I'd jump to slag off his breeks –
With him still dressed up in his Sunday best –
But I just stood my ground and held my breath,
For he'd been in the grave for seven weeks.

Early Morning Prayer Meeting

(Glengormley, 1988)

O Lord,

if it be your will
that Northern Ireland
remain part of the United Kingdom,
separate from the rest of Ireland,
let it be so, O Lord

Amen, brother! Amen!

O Lord,

if it be your will
that Northern Ireland
be separate from the United Kingdom
and from the rest of Ireland,
let it be so, O Lord

Amen, brother!

O Lord,

if it be your will
that Northern Ireland
be joined with the rest of Ireland
and be separate from the United Kingdom,
let it be so, O Lord

(Silence)

Roman

The oldies are dancing
In Whitehouse Working Men's Club,
Circling the floor in twos

Like characters on a carousel.
A lady stalwart announces
The deaths of two more (ex)

Members since last week.
The bar theme is Roman.
There's a guy – medals on – singing.

Distance

Sometimes
most times

the distance
is too far

Like trying
to touch

your own face
in the mirror

The Right Word

for Larry Monteith

Put your ears to the trees ... what can you hear?
Children and teachers move in to listen,
Touching each trunk like there's something to fear,
Their faces full of anticipation.
Then the shock as everyone fathoms
The hidden melody of living trees,
That sounds like they hold tremendous gallons
Thundering into invisible seas.
Both teachers and children gather themselves
To pen a few words to frame for the shelves
And walls of their classrooms and families.
One tough guy checks it was water he heard –
Same water that rolls through you and through me –
Then moves on, chuffed that he knew the right word.

Closer

for Dorothy Maguire

Every day
we go farther away

from that
which we once knew

But don't dismay
for as we do

we grow closer to
the memory of it

Related

for Brian Murphy (1949-2014)

'Thran' –
A classic Ulsterism:
Stubborn, contrary, cross-grained.

Personally, I'm convinced
It comes from 'Thracian' –
A Roman racehorse,

Untouchable, barbarian.
True or false, there's me,
Standing at a bar toilet-trough

In rural Mullaghbawn,
Lined up alongside a posse
Of smiling old men:

We believe you're related to
Our big man?

I am.

That's good, that's good …
Though we trust you're not as ……

Thran?

The Other Side

for Matthew Rice (1906-1964)

Scanning my Catholic
granda's Mass card,
suddenly death
seems more exciting,
the natural next step.

We have loved him in life; let us
not forget him in death.

From St. Ambrose,
who lay in his cradle
dribbled with honey
from bees who had
blessed him with
their liquid gold,
giving his father
some high hopes
for his eloquence
and honeyed tongue.

Then there's 'Ambrosia',
the nectar of the gods.
And then there's
'Ambrosia Creamed Rice',
the tinned working-class dish
we had to enjoy – urban
frogspawn, the cheap clotted
water of working-class life.

We have loved him in life; let us
not forget him in death.

And let us not forget the storm and the strife.

Against the Sun

When angry fathers
Raised their hands

Against the sun,
Hairs on their forearms

Were warriors

Gathering along
The ridge-flesh of bone.

Pre-Texts

If you eat the crusts of the Ormo plain,
your hair will be lovely and curly.

Don't put money in your mouth
or you'll choke and die.

You are no better than anyone,
and no-one is any better than you.

Don't ever ink your skin
or it will poison you.

Try to hold your wheest.

You'll get square eyes if you sit
too long in front of the TV.

Always check the apple for the bee.

If you're not careful,
you'll turn out like your Da.

Hap up or you'll catch your death of cold.

Never go out without clean underpants
and socks, for anything could happen
to you, and you wouldn't want to end
up in the hospital or the ditch, embarrassed.

Always watch the road.

Charis

Just ten, you crossed
The Atlantic on your own.
Just to be with me.

Every hair on your
Head was ringlet.
Your face shone.

You made sure
That you did your
Holiday homework,

Even then. Even alone.
I knew then that you'd
Go far, on your own.

But the thing that I
Remember most,
The most precious,

Is our trips
To the downtown
Dundas arcade.

Your eyes lit up,
Like mine, every time
We would set out.

And having nothing,
We still had all –
A bag of silver

Change as heavy
As a cannon ball.
Like we'd found,

Together,
The bottom
Of the wishing well.

'Charis'.
God's grace.
Unmerited favour.

Just ten, you crossed
The Atlantic on your own.
Just to be with me.

Throwaway

for Charlotte

It's the night-sleeve
That I sleep in,
My Irish simmit.

It covers my chest,
Shrouds the strange forest
Of my midnight ribs;

Drapes from my shoulders,
A black cotton curtain
You can't see through,

But she sees through
To my fatherly heart,
Her human home.

She doesn't want me
To ever take it off.
But even she knows

That one day soon
It will needs be
A throwaway.

The Fated Hour

for Kenneth Robert Rice (1938-2014)

> *Thou hast felt*
> *What 'tis to die and live again before*
> *Thy fated hour.*
>
> – John Keats, 'Hyperion: A Vision'

Over my father
Hangs
The fated hour.

I know that I
Will be unable
To proffer proper

Consolation,
In person, but
I am trying, vainly,

To hold his hand
By phone;
A hand as once

As squat
And four-square
As my very own:

Palm-proud,
Knuckle-bright,
Fist-sure –

The hand
He gave me
When I was born.

And gave me,
As a child,
When I would fall.

A hand that was also
Too ready, on occasion,
To set me straight;

The same hand that
Kept me from harm,
For 'One Punch Ken'

Was nobody's doll,
Even in Rathcoole:
Hurt me, hurt us,

You hurt all.
Comforting cliché,
I see him in the mirror,

And feel him in my hand.
Psalmist! Oul Psalmist!
Everything now is

That old sinking sand.

'Adrain'

Dad, on that last day,
as I pictured you
aflame,

one of the saddest
thoughts that came
to me was –

only Mum will spell my
name wrong,
now that you

are gone.

Consolation

Our old front door whinnies open.
Spring has come, though
nothing too flowery
is, as yet, on show.
But, in faith,
we know it's happening,
the temporal return.

I can see that nature
has been trimmed.
Trees and big shrubs
have been cut back
to mollycoddle cables,
and more sky comes through,
which is some small mercy.

The trimmed trees and shrubs –
what more can they do
but keep on coming?
There will be no surrender.
We will not be tamed.

Our neighbour pulls in
in her car, and points
at me on the porch,
with a, *Ah, I see it's*
now all right with the world!
I could send her the very same back.

So the sun still goes down,
and the night still comes on slow,
salving us with natural shadow.
And neighbours move, once more,
with shadows along the evening avenue.

It has been a year since my dad disappeared.
So, every spring will be his yearly requiem.
We didn't plan it. But then again,
it's no real surprise that spring
has sprung with such a consolation.

Without Fail

for Nana Jean

Without fail, every time I try to (kind of) proudly present
my mother with my latest publication, she feigns interest

in the paper thing, and shyly backhands it, with a blushful grin,
to whoever is seated closest to her, to whom she submits:

Would you mind just putting that up there on the shelf with the others?
And then, pretending I'm not in the room, she further confesses,

truthfully, towards their innocent ear: *You know, I'll not read that.*

If I could remember all at once – but I have forgotten.
Still, some day, looking along a furrowed cliff, staring
Beyond the eyes' strength, I'll start an avalanche,
And every stone will fall separate and revealed ...

from 'Meditation' by William Stafford

Adrian Rice is from Northern Ireland. He was born just north of Belfast in 1958, in Whitehouse, Newtownabbey, County Antrim. He graduated from the University of Ulster with a BA in English & Politics, and MPhil in Anglo-Irish Literature. He has delivered writing workshops, readings, and lectures throughout the UK & Ireland, and America. His first sequence of poems appeared in *Muck Island* (Moongate Publications, 1990), a collaboration with leading Irish artist, Ross Wilson. Copies of this limited edition box-set are housed in the collections of The Tate Gallery, The Boston Museum of Fine Arts, and The Lamont Library at Harvard University. A following chapbook, *Impediments* (Abbey Press, 1997), also earned widespread critical acclaim. He edited *Signals* (Abbey Press, 1997), which was a London *Times Educational Supplement* 'Paperback Choice'. He has also edited five anthologies of children's poetry, art and drama. In 1997, Rice received the Sir James Kilfedder Memorial Bursary for Emerging Artists. In autumn 1999, as recipient of the US/Ireland Exchange Bursary, he was Poet-in-Residence at Lenoir-Rhyne College, Hickory, NC, where he received 'The Key to the City'. His first full poetry collection – *The Mason's Tongue* (Abbey Press, 1999) – was shortlisted for the Christopher Ewart-Biggs Memorial Literary Prize, nominated for the Irish Times Prize for Poetry, and translated into Hungarian by Thomas Kabdebo (*A Komuves Nyelve*, epl/ediotio plurilingua, 2005). In 2002, he co-edited a major Irish anthology entitled, *A Conversation Piece: Poetry and Art* (The Ulster Museum in association with Abbey Press). His publications also include *The Tin God*, a history of Cans Metal Box factory, Portadown, which was shortlisted for the 'Celebrating Our Local History' Competition by the Northern Ireland Publications Resource; and *Insights* (as editor), an anthology of poetry from The

Dungannon Visually-Impaired Group, which earned the Dungannon & South Tyrone Borough Council's 'Achievement Award'. His poems and reviews have been broadcast internationally on radio and television, and have been published in several international magazines and journals, including *Poetry Ireland Review* and *The New Orleans Review*. Selections of his poetry and prose have appeared in both *The Belfast Anthology* and *The Ulster Anthology* (Ed., Patricia Craig, Blackstaff Press, 1999 & 2006) and in *Magnetic North: The Emerging Poets* (Ed., John Brown, Lagan Press, 2006). A chapbook, *Hickory Haiku*, was published in 2010 by Finishing Line Press, Kentucky. Rice returned to Lenoir-Rhyne College as Visiting Writer-in-Residence for 2005. Since then, Adrian and his poet-wife Molly, and young son, Micah, have settled in Hickory, from where he now commutes to Boone for Doctoral studies at Appalachian State University. Turning poetry into lyrics, he has also teamed up with Hickory-based and fellow Belfastman, musician/songwriter Alyn Mearns, to form 'The Belfast Boys', a dynamic Irish Traditional Music duo. Their debut album, *Songs For Crying Out Loud*, was released in 2010. Adrian's last book, *The Clock Flower*, was first published by Moongate Publications (Northern Ireland, 2012) in a limited edition, and then re-released in an extended American edition by Press 53, in 2013.

Cover photographer Alan Mearns is a poet-songwriter originally from Belfast, Northern Ireland. Now rooted with his family in the foothills of the North Carolina Appalachian Mountains, he performs his songs under the moniker 'Yes the Raven', and performs traditional Irish music as one half of 'The Belfast Boys'.